FAMILY CRAFTING
Fun Projects to Do Together

Carol Scheffler

Sterling Publishing Co., Inc. New York
A Sterling/Chapelle Book

Chapelle Ltd.

Owner
Jo Packham

Editor
Karmen Quinney

Staff
Marie Barber, Ann Bear, Areta Bingham,
Kass Burchett, Rebecca Christensen,
Marilyn Goff, Holly Hollingsworth,
Susan Jorgensen, Barbara Milburn, Linda Orton,
Leslie Ridenour, Cindy Stoeckl, Gina Swapp

Photographer
Kevin Dilley/Hazen Photography Studio

Model
Rachel Stoeckl

Library of Congress Cataloging-in-Publication Data

Scheffler, Carol.
    Family crafting : fun projects to do together / Carol Scheffler
        p. cm.
    "A Sterling/Chapelle Book"
    Includes index.
    ISBN 0-8069-2899-9
    1. Handicraft. I. Title.

TT157.S32 2000   99-087165
745.5—dc21

10 9 8 7 6 5 4 3 2 1

First paperback edition published 2001 by
Sterling Publishing Company, Inc.,
387 Park Avenue South, New York, NY 10016
© 2000 by Chapelle Limited
Distributed in Canada by Sterling Publishing
C/o Canadian Manda Group, One Atlantic Avenue, Suite 105
Toronto, Ontario, Canada M6K 3E7
Distributed in Great Britain and Europe by Cassell PLC
Wellington House, 125 Strand, London WC2R 0BB, England
Distributed in Australia by Capricorn Link (Australia) Pty. Ltd.
P.O. Box 704, Windsor, NSW 2756 Australia

Printed in China
All Rights Reserved

Sterling ISBN 0-8069-2899-9 Trade
            0-8069-2898-0 Paper

If you have any questions or comments, please contact:
Chapelle Ltd., Inc., P. O. Box 9252 Ogden, UT 84409
(801) 621-2777 • FAX (801) 621-2788 • e-mail: Chapelle@
Chapelleltd.com • website: www.chapelleltd.com

FAMILY CRAFTING
Fun Projects
to Do Together

About the Author

Widely recognized as one of today's leading arts and craft experts, Carol Scheffler's advice to crafters can be found in every popular forum—network and cable television, national magazines, newspapers, books, and leading crafts and media websites.

Carol is the Arts and Crafts Contributor to NBC's TODAY SHOW, presenting the most exciting trends in crafts and home decor to Katie Couric, Matt Lauer, and the show's viewers around the world. She also appears regularly on the Discovery Channel, HGTV, and public television's Hands on Crafts for Kids.

Carol is very proud of her role as the Arts and Crafts Editor of *Parents Magazine*, bringing innovative and fun family crafting projects into the homes of millions of readers each month. Carol also writes and designs for other national magazines, including *McCall's* and *Better Homes and Gardens Crafts and Decorating Showcase*.

In Carol's book, *Rubber Stamping for the First Time*, she teaches the beginning rubber stamper how to make great looking projects with ease and style.

Carol shares her crafting tips and views on the latest trends through her articles and projects on IdeaForest.com.

Carol is delighted to serve as the Spokesperson for National Craft Month, observed in March each year to celebrate the joys of crafting.

Carol's daughters, Madeline (13), Eliza (10), and Susannah (6), and husband, Michael, are Carol's favorite family crafting partners. They reside in Larchmont, New York.

Dedication

I dedicate this book to the many thousands of people to whom I have taught crafting. As is often the case, the pupils have taught the teacher . . . that the love of creating is something that everyone shares, regardless of gender or age; that directions should be followed only when they help you achieve your vision and should be thrown out the window when they don't; that there is no such thing as "talented" or "untalented," there is only the courage to jump in with both feet and give a new project a try. As a teacher, my favorite six words in the English language are "Wow, look what I just made!", because I know my

student surprised herself with her accomplishment.

I also dedicate this book to my daughters, Madeline, Eliza, and Susannah, and my husband, Michael, who have given me the freedom, inspiration, and support to allow me to follow my dreams.

Acknowledgment

Publishing a book successfully is an enormous task, accomplished only by dedicated and talented people with a real commitment to making the author's vision a reality. I was lucky to have worked with such people. I would like to acknowledge and thank Jo Packham, Karmen Quinney, and Kass Burchett at Chapelle Ltd.; Lincoln Boehm, Charles Nurnberg, and Chris Vaccari at Sterling Publishing; and all my other friends at Chapelle and Sterling.

What's Inside

Note to Parents

Design-a-Stamp Gift Wrap

Welcome to *Family Crafting*. My goal is to provide you and your family with a wealth of ideas for crafting projects, inspiring you to have fun together and create "great stuff," as my kids would say. I find that when our family gathers together to craft, we all relax, learn a little more about each other, enjoy the cooperative effort, and have lots of laughs. Somehow, when hands are busy, conversation naturally starts to flow and you have a chance to catch up on each other's lives. The rewards are immeasurable—not only will you share pride in the project you have created together, but you will also have produced lasting memories of fun family times.

Perhaps you are wondering, "What exactly is family crafting?" Family crafting is an approach to crafting with children that encourages adults to be involved in the process. For the most part, the projects in this book are designed so that children can make them almost entirely by themselves, if they want to. However, instead of just providing your child with materials and leaving them alone to work independently, family crafting is an opportunity to participate in a project with your child, at any level that is comfortable for both of you. One child may rarely ask for help. Another child may lean on you more heavily for guidance. Of course, age and experience will both be factors. Take the cue from your child to determine the desired level of assistance. Occasionally, there may be a step which only a grown-up can perform for safety reasons. I will note those steps with the following symbol in the project directions:♥.

There is one paramount rule of family crafting: Do not take over your children's work and do it for them. They will assume that they are doing it "wrong" and their creativity will stop flowing. Instead, assemble an extra set of materials so that you can make your own project while your children make theirs. That way, you will be working together, while still allowing your children's creativity to flourish.

(Besides, you know you're going to want to get in on the fun, too!)

This book is filled with projects that are great looking as well as functional. Thus, any one of these projects can be turned into an attractive gift for a special occasion. When children make a present themselves, they feel more involved in the particular holiday or celebration. This gives them an enormous sense of pride and accomplishment. Also, your child will learn from the recipient's reaction that there is no gift more wonderful than one made by the hand and from the heart.

Creative Environment

Contrary to popular thought, creativity and structure do go hand in hand.

When:

• Pick a convenient time to work on a project.

• Make certain you have at least 45 relatively uninterrupted minutes. You will be able to finish just about any one of the projects in this book within that time-frame. There is nothing more frustrating than beginning the creative process and then having to stop soon after beginning.

Where:

• Select a place to work where you won't ruin anything (like carpeting).

• Make certain you spread out your materials so that they are within reach.

• Cover your work surface with an old plastic tablecloth or newspapers.

Travel Board Game

• Use empty plastic containers to hold paint or glue and plastic lids as palettes. Scissors should be placed with the blades down in an empty container.

• Keep markers, crayons, and colored pencils in separate containers.

9

• Craft sticks or expired credit cards make effective tools for spreading glue or flattening fabric or paper once it has been glued.

• Remember to explain to your children that cleaning up is an important step in any creative process. Everyone who works on the project is responsible for cleaning up.

• Wash brushes thoroughly and sort and return materials to their containers.

• Store partially completed projects, as well as fabrics, trims, and papers, in a dry, safe area.

• Clean the work surface and floor.

What:

• I have chosen materials that are inexpensive and readily available in craft, fabric, and general merchandise stores. You probably have many materials in your home right now. In addition, some of the projects employ items that are generally recycled or discarded, demonstrating that beauty and function can be found in even the most mundane objects.

• I have used a wide variety of techniques, including decoupage, painting, collage, sewing, quilting, and nature printing, to name a few. I have also provided some background

Polar Fleece Scarf & Hat

information, including how, why, and where certain crafts first originated, so that your children will gain an appreciation for the history of the craft.

• Encourage your children to think beyond what they see pictured. For instance, if your children would like to make the **Polar Fleece Scarf & Hat** above, but don't like red, help them to understand that they can pick any color fabric that appeals to them. If they do not like ribbon and button embellishments, they can leave them off or substitute others. Reinforce the idea that they, not you or I, are the designers of the projects.

Nurture Creativity

The best way to nurture creativity in your child is to observe and impart a few basic principles:

• Creating is a process that occasionally produces surprises, problems to solve, and unexpected outcomes. Sometimes we follow a direction and the results are not what we envisioned. This does not make it wrong.

• Take a "mistake" and try to make it work towards achieving your vision. Mistakes often turn into wonderful discoveries. Most of all, have fun! There are very few rights and wrongs in crafting. If it pleases you, then it is "right."

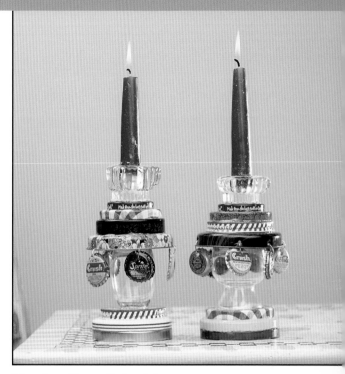

Funky Candleholders

• Appreciate your children's work. When they finish a project, use it, wear it, display it, play with it, and share it. Celebrate their accomplishment.

• Take your children to museums and galleries.

• Open their eyes and imagination to art in the world around them. Help your children notice outdoor sculpture or interesting decor in a restaurant or shop. Ask them what they like about it or find pleasing. This enables them to develop their own sense of color, scale, texture, pattern, and dimension.

I hope you will find inspiration in the ideas presented here. I wish you and your family many happy hours creating and learning together and enjoying each other's company.

Carol Scheffler

Note to Kids

Treasure Mirror

Dear Kids,

I am so excited to be sharing this book with you! I designed the projects so that you and your family would have fun working on them together. Also, you can make some really useful things . . . like a clock for your room, a box to hold your baseball cards, a game to play on your next family trip, or a pretty candle to give as a gift.

You'll see that I give you directions to make each project the way it is shown in the photograph. However, you are the designer of the project —not me! If you like the winter scarf and hat, but red just isn't your color—pick a different color fabric. Part of the fun of crafting is designing the project yourself.

Crafting is always more successful if everyone follows a few rules:

• Ask a grown-up if this is a good time to begin a project.

• Gather your supplies, so that they are handy.

• Cover the work surface with newspaper or an old plastic tablecloth.

• Cover your clothes with an old shirt or smock.

• Tie back your hair if it is long.

• Place caps back on glue and paint containers right away so that they won't spill or dry out.

• Clean up spills and dribbles as you go along.

• When you are finished, put everything back into its container and wash off the table and floor.

• If your project isn't done or needs to dry, ask a grown-up where you should keep it so that it will be safely out of the way.

• Never put any crafting supplies in your mouth. Always be especially careful with scissors and craft knives.

Safety is very important in all projects. I have marked certain steps in the directions with this symbol: 💜. It means that a grown-up needs to help you with this step.

Example:

💜 **3** Using hammer and nail, make six evenly spaced holes around rim of largest remaining lid. Make one hole in center of each bottle cap.

Following these simple rules will make your crafting time safer, more productive, and more FUN.

Have a wonderful time making these projects!

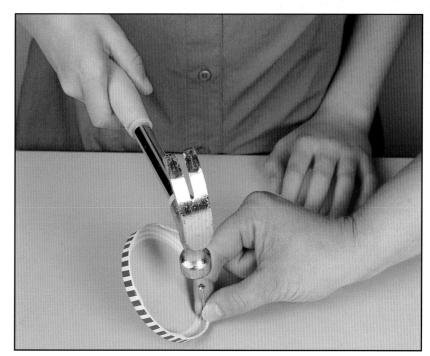

Step 3

13

Basics

While some of the projects in this book call for specific materials that you may need to purchase at a craft store, most of the projects rely on supplies you probably already have in your home, such as craft punches, glue, markers, scissors, tape, tape measure, etc.

Glue

Glue comes in many different types. Use the type of glue that best fits the project. When using any type of glue, make sure to keep glue lines clean and neat.

Cement glue—used for gluing odd-shaped items to most surfaces

Craft glue—used for general gluing (available in liquid or stick form)

Decoupage glue—used as a glue, sealer, and finisher

Fabric glue—used for fabrics

Wood glue—used for woods

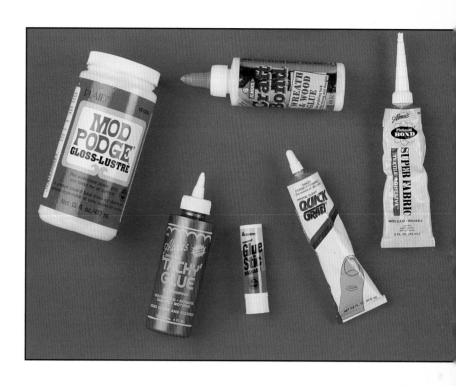

Measuring Boxes

You will need a tape measure, pencil, and a piece of paper to write down the measurements.

1. Measure height of box (A).

2. Write this measurement down.

3. Starting at one corner, measure all the way around box (B).

4. Write this measurement down.

5. Cut paper to fit these measurements.

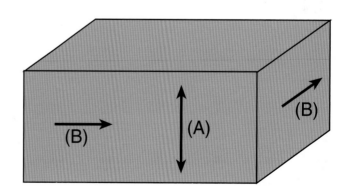

Rubber Stamping

You will need a rubber stamp, marker, and surface to print the image on.

1. Hold the stamp, rubber side up, with one hand.

2. Ink the stamp by holding the marker in your other hand and brushing it against the raised part of the rubber die, using the side of the marker, not the tip.

Steps 1–2

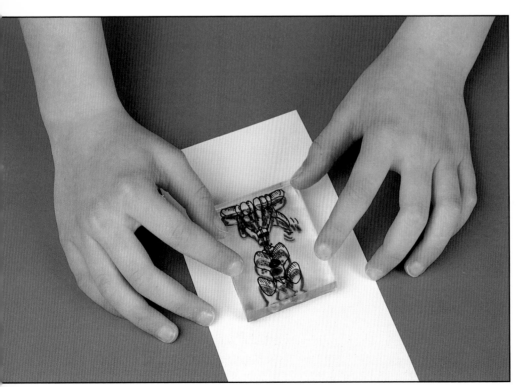

3. Print the image by placing the stamp, rubber die side down, onto the surface. Without rocking or twisting the stamp, give it a little pressure.

4. Lift stamp straight up off surface. Allow ink to dry.

Step 3

Scissors

Scissors come in many different types. Each type of scissor is used for a different reason.

(1) Decorative-edged scissors— used for cutting colored papers and card stock in a wide range of styles. These scissors have two directions of edges, depending on how you hold them.

(2) Fabric scissors—used for cutting fabrics, ribbons, and thread. They should not be used on paper or any other craft items.

(3) Craft scissors—used for cutting paper and other craft items.

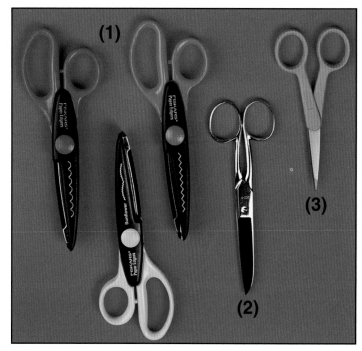

Scissors

Step 1

1. Position decorative-edged scissors in your hand so the desired edge will cut.

2. Trim paper as desired, matching up the edge of the design with each cut of the scissors.

Holidays

Valentine Jewelry

"Charm" everyone with this matching shrink plastic charm bracelet and earrings set that has "Be My Valentine" written all over it. Shrink plastic is easy to work with and amazing to watch as it curls, twists, then shrinks flat before your eyes. Let the jewelry making begin .

What You Need

Aluminum foil

Craft scissors

Eye pins: 2" (2)

Gold jump rings: 12 mm (9)

Gold link bracelet

Hole punch: ¼"

Large craft punch: heart-
shaped

Oven mitts

Red bugle beads (4)

Red permanent marker

Round-nose pliers

Sandpaper: 400–500 grit
(1 sheet)

Small white beads (13)

Toaster oven with tray

Translucent shrink plastic
(1 sheet)

Wire cutters

Wire earring loops (2)

What You Need

What to Do

1 Sand sheet of shrink plastic crosswise and lengthwise.

2 Place shrink plastic vertically on work surface. Using craft punch, punch nine hearts from bottom of shrink plastic sheet. Using craft scissors, cut off edge of plastic sheet where row of hearts has been punched. Be sure to cut a straight edge.

Step 2

3 Using hole punch, punch hole in upper right-hand corner of each heart.

4 Using marker, color both sides and edge of each heart. Let ink dry for five minutes.

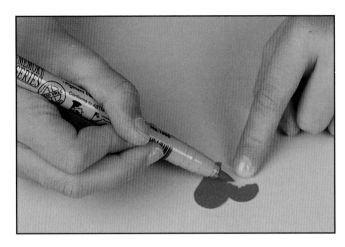

Step 4

5 Preheat toaster oven to 275°. Line tray of toaster oven with aluminum foil. Place hearts on tray.

6 Bake for 2–3 minutes. Do not let hearts touch while baking. *As hearts heat up, curling and shrinking will occur. Eventually hearts will lie flat. This means that they are fully baked.* Using oven mitts, remove tray from toaster oven. Let hearts cool on tray for five minutes.

7 Thread one white bead and one red bead onto eye pin. Repeat for remaining eye pin.

8 Using wire cutters, cut off ¾" from eye pin. Using round-nose pliers, curl end of eye pin closed around earring loop.

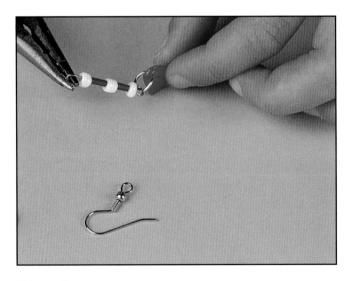

Step 8

20

9 Open jump ring by pulling one end toward you while pushing other end away from you. *Don't pull ends apart because this will weaken jump ring, causing it to break.*

10 Thread jump ring through heart charm and bottom of eye pin. Close jump ring. Repeat for other earring.

11 Open jump ring as in Step 9. Thread heart charm and white bead onto jump ring. Thread open jump ring through link in bracelet. Close jump ring. Space seven hearts around bracelet.

Valentine's Day Coupon Book

A
Valentine's Day
Coupon Book

For You

Here's a new way to send Valentine's greetings to some-one special. Place personalized coupons in festive envelopes inside this Valentine's Day Coupon Book, to be traded in by the lucky person who receives this gift on Valentine's Day. Use this idea to make a coupon book as a unique birthday present. **21**

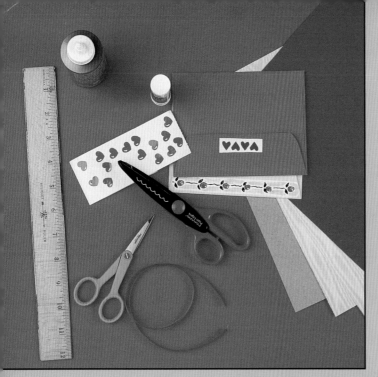

What You Need

What to Do

1 Place pink papers, right side down on work surface. Glue one cardboard piece onto center of each pink paper.

2 Trim off corners of paper.

3 Apply glue to overhanging pieces of pink paper and fold onto cardboard.

Step 3

22

4 Place covered cardboard pieces ¼" apart, wrong side up and side by side, on work surface.

5 Apply glue in a thin horizontal line across center of each cardboard piece from one side to the other. Center ribbon onto glue line. Leave ends of ribbon lying flat on work surface.

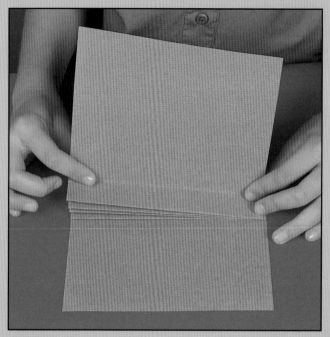

Step 6

6 Measure 6" from end of construction paper and fold. Keep folding paper, making ¾" accordion pleats. Make four complete accordion pleats. *There should be a 6" portion of construction paper remaining on each side of the accordion pleats.*

7 Turn over construction paper. Glue one 6" portion onto center of each cardboard piece. Let dry for 30 minutes.

8 Glue four envelopes, flap side up and out, onto accordion pleats. Glue fifth envelope onto inside of back cover of book. Starting with pink envelope, change color of envelopes each time.

Step 8

23

9 Decorate envelopes with stickers.

10 Using black marker, create title for book on decorative paper. Using scallop-edged scissors, cut out title. Apply glue to title and place onto piece of dark red decorative paper.

11 Using scallop-edged scissors, trim dark red paper. Glue title onto center of book. Decorate title with stickers.

12 Make handwritten **Coupons** with decorative paper. Decorate with stickers. Insert coupons into each envelope.

13 Tie coupon book closed with ribbon.

Coupons—write down any chore or special act that you can do for someone else. For example: *A Free Hug!*; *Good for one week of doing dishes*; or *Good for vacuuming the living room.*

Good for one week of doing the dishes.

Good for one free HUG

Good for vacuuming the living room.

CD Case Photo Frames

Hang your favorite snapshots in special frames made from compact disk cases, ribbon, and a soda can pop-top. These frames would also make great gifts for friends or family.

What You Need

Compact disk cases (2)

Craft glue

Craft scissors

Grosgrain ribbons, 1"-wide:
  red (15")
  red polka-dot (48")

Ribbon roses: large (8)

Ruler

Soda can pop-top

What You Need

What to Do

1 Cut four 5½" pieces and four 5" pieces from red polka-dot ribbon.

2 Apply glue to backs of ribbon pieces. Place one 5½" piece of ribbon onto each side of case. Place one 5" piece of ribbon onto top and bottom of cases, over-lapping ends. Let dry for one hour.

3 Place cases, front side down, vertically 1½" apart on table. Glue 15" piece of red ribbon onto center of cases, starting 1" down from top edge of first case.

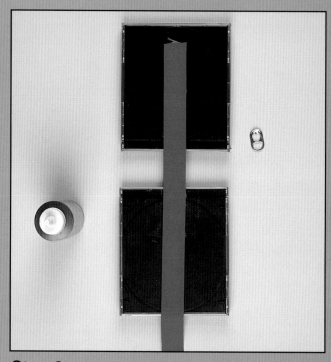

Step 3

4 Cut small v-shape at bottom end of ribbon.

5 Glue soda can pop-top onto back of case at top of ribbon, extending half over top of case. Let glue dry for one hour. desired. *Rubber cement can be used if a greater strength of glue is desired.*

6 Glue one ribbon rose onto each front corner. Let dry for one hour.

7 Place pictures inside cases. *You've just created beautiful picture frames.*

Step 6–7

Check This Out: Craft projects that incorporate materials which would ordinarily be thrown away are a great idea! This reduces garbage and, at the same time, makes the project more unique.

Did you know that . . . .

An aluminum can that is thrown away will continue to clutter the landscape for at least 500 years.

A glass bottle would still be there in the year 3000.

Every time you recycle a glass bottle, you save enough energy to light a 100 Watt light bulb for four hours, which is the amount of electricity consumed in making a new glass bottle.

Plastics are now being recycled into carpeting, polar fleece fabric, stuffing in sleeping bags, and garden supplies, just to name few items.

So, let your crafting projects also be a recycling one!

27

Easter Flowerpots

Button flowers are always blooming in these charming flower-pots, even on rainy days. They will help make any springtime celebration special!

Check This Out: Set flowerpots on the table as a centerpiece and spread jelly beans around them. You could make one for each guest and write their names on it, serving as a place card as well as a table decoration.

What You Need

What You Need (for one)

Acrylic paints: light blue; pink; white; yellow

Black permanent marker

Buttons: assorted shapes; assorted colors

Craft glue

Craft scissors

Floral foam or Styrofoam®

Floral tape

Floral wire

Kitchen knife

Pastel Easter grass

Pencil with eraser

Silk leaves

Sponge brush

Tape measure

Terra-cotta pot: 3"

What to Do

1 Thread a piece of floral wire from bottom of button, through hole and back down from top of button through another hole.

2 Bring ends together, making them even. Twist wire several times directly under button to hold it in place. Using craft scissors, cut wire, measuring 5".

3 Tightly twist floral tape around top of wire under button. After 1" of wire has been covered, hold silk leaf stem on floral wire and twist floral tape over stem, attaching it to wire. Keep twisting floral tape until the whole wire is covered. Cut off extra floral tape.

Step 3

4 Repeat Steps 1–3 for desired number of flowers.

5 Using sponge brush, paint each pot with two coats of desired color of paint. Let dry for 30 minutes.

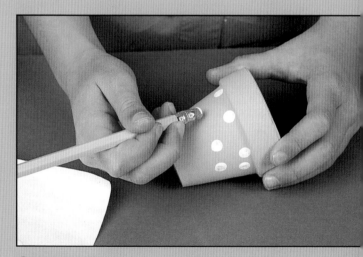

Step 6

6 Dip pencil eraser into white paint. Press eraser on pot, making sure dots are solid. Redip eraser into paint and press as necessary. Let dry for 30 minutes.

7 Using marker, write an Easter message along rim of pot.

8 Using kitchen knife, cut floral foam or Styrofoam® piece to fit into bottom of pot. Place cut floral foam or Styrofoam® into pot.

9 Glue grass onto top of floral foam or Styrofoam®, making sure it sticks out above pot rim.

10 Push each flower into floral foam or Styrofoam®. Arrange flowers and leaves as desired, making sure they look full.

Patchwork Easter Eggs

The Easter bunny would love to discover beautiful patterned eggs like these. Hunt for fabric scraps, buttons, and ribbons around the house to make these patchwork eggs.

What You Need

Craft glue

Fabric scissors

Foam eggs

Pastel patterned fabrics: assorted

Pastel ribbons: assorted

Pastel ribbon roses: assorted

Pastel rickrack: assorted

Small pastel buttons: assorted

Straight pins

What to Do

1 Cut out odd-shaped pieces at least 1" in diameter from different patterned fabrics.

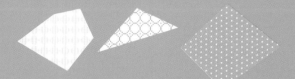

Ideas for Shapes

2 Place one piece of fabric on egg. Pin corners down, pushing pins into egg.

3 Place next piece of fabric, overlapping one side of first piece. Pin fabric in place, pushing pins into egg. Keep adding and pinning fabric pieces until the whole egg is covered.

Step 3

4 Cut ribbons and rick-racks to cover edges of fabric, using different lengths as needed.

5 Run thin line of glue over seam line where fabrics overlap. Place ribbon or rickrack onto each seam line until all seams are covered. Let dry for one hour.

Step 5

6 Glue buttons where several ribbon or rickrack pieces meet.

7 Using tip of fabric scissors, make small hole in top of egg.

8 Cut 6" piece of ribbon. Fold in half. Place glue in hole and push end of handle inside hole. *You've just created a handle.* Let dry for one hour.

9 Cut two 12" pieces of ribbon. Holding ribbon pieces together, tie into bow. Glue bow onto egg at base of ribbon loop handle.

10 Glue ribbon rose onto center of bow. Let dry for one hour.

Check This Out: Eggs have always represented rebirth and new beginnings, a perfect symbol for Spring. Every European country has their own way of decorating eggs. For example, in Greece, eggs are dyed dark red; in the Ukraine and the Czech Republic, eggs are batiked, using hot wax. People from Poland introduced the idea of decorating eggs with cut and colored paper. People all over the world have enjoyed decorating eggs in a wide variety of ways.

Halloween Ghouls

Hang these spooky creatures all around the house to let everyone know "This place is haunted!" Gather some felt, glue, wire hangers, and some of Mom's old panty hose. Let the ghoulish fun begin!

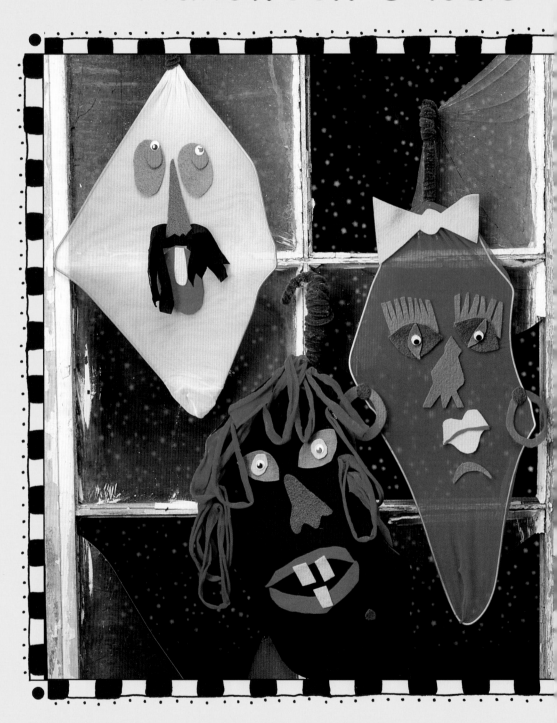

Hang ghouls, peeking through tree branches and stair railings, and over doorways. Try gluing on heavy string and use as masks. You can see right through them.

What You Need (for one)

Craft glue

Craft scissors

Craft sticks

Felt scraps: assorted colors

Googly eyes

Panty hose

Pipe cleaners

Wire hanger

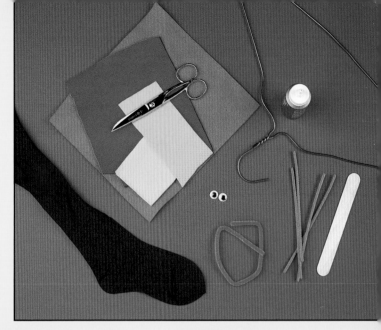

What You Need

What to Do

1 Pull wire hanger into desired shape for ghoul's face. Hanger hook will be at top of head.

2 Insert hanger, "chin" first, into one leg of panty hose. Cut off panty hose 1" above hanger hook. Tie top 3" into a knot at base of hook. Tuck extra fabric back into knot.

3 Wrap pipe cleaners around entire hook, covering knot.

4 Cut facial features from felt scraps. Make eyes, nose and mouths irregular and oversized. *This will add personality to your ghoul.*

Step 2

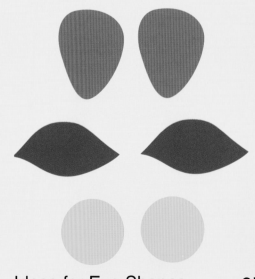

Ideas for Eye Shapes

5 Using craft stick, apply glue onto back of each facial feature. Place onto panty hose as desired. *Try gluing felt scraps lopsided for a scary look.* Let glue dry for 30 minutes.

6 See **Hair** or **Mustache**, if desired.

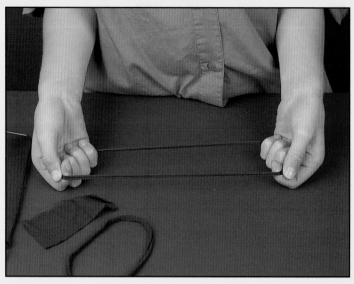

Step 6

Hair

1. Cut several 1"-wide strips across leg of panty hose.

2. Place hand into circle of fabric and stretch it out. Glue onto top and around facial features.

Mustache

1. Cut several ½"-wide strips across leg of panty hose, then cut each circle open.

2. Glue center of pieces lengthwise under ghoul's nose.

36

Slinky Slithery Snakes

These bendable reptiles look great twisted around your bedpost or over a mirror. They can also sit silently in the corner, ready to strike. For a quick costume, loop one over your shoulder, add a turban, and you're now a snake charmer. Look closely and see if you can guess what they're made of.

What You Need (for one)

Craft glue

Fabric scissors

Felt scraps: assorted colors

Matching thread

Necktie

Needle

Polyester filling

Ruler or long stick

Wire hanger

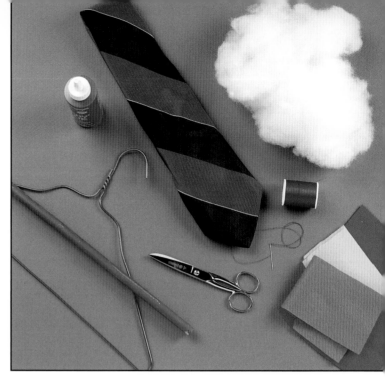

What You Need

Step 1

What to Do

♥1 Untwist wire hanger, making it as straight as possible. Feed wire hanger through entire length of necktie. *If hanger catches on any small stitches inside the tie, use scissors to cut stitches open.*

2 Push small bunches of polyester filling into tie from both ends. *If stuffed with large bunches, the snake will look lumpy.* Using ruler or stick, push polyester filling deep into center of tie, gathering tie as necessary. Keep stuffing until the whole tie is filled.

Step 2

3 Using needle and thread, **Whipstitch** both ends of tie closed.

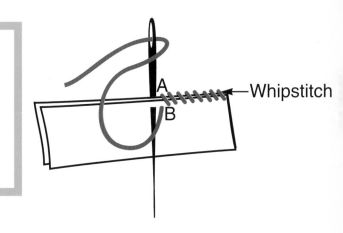

Whipstitch

1. Bring needle up at A; taking a small stitch. Slide needle through folded edge of fabric about ⅛" to ¼" and out at B.

2. Repeat until seam is closed.

4 Cut out desired shapes for eyes and tongue from felt scraps.

5 Glue eyes and tongue onto front side of large end of tie. Let dry for several hours.

6 Shape snake by twisting as desired.

Ideas for Eye and Tongue Shapes

This spooky trick-or-treat bucket will hold your loot for many Halloweens to come. Create these creepy designs with compressed sponges that you design and cut out.

Trick-or-Treat Bucket

What You Need

Acrylic paints: orange; white; yellow

Aluminum foil

Black spray paint

Compressed sponges

Craft scissors

Fabric strips: 1" x 18"; 1" x 8" (2)

Hole punch: ¼"

Metal paint bucket

Paint markers: orange; white; yellow

Pencil

Spray metal primer

Water

What You Need

What to Do

1 In a well-ventilated area, spray bucket with metal primer, following manufacturer's instructions. Let dry for 15 minutes.

2 Spray-paint bucket black. Let dry for one hour.

3 Using pencil, sketch ghost, star, and "Boo" on sponge. Cut out images. *The hole punch is terrific for creating eyes on ghost or circles in middle of "B" or "o"s in "Boo".*

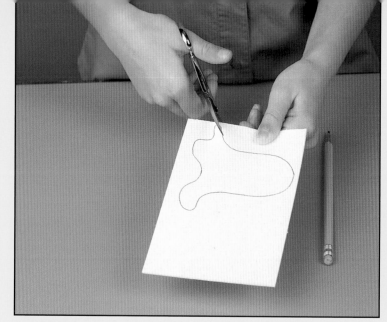

Step 3

4 Using water, dampen sponge images, making them puff up. Pour small amount of white acrylic paint onto aluminum foil. Tap sponge ghost image into paint until fully covered. Place sponge onto bucket and gently walk your fingers over sponge until image is transferred. *Several more ghosts can be printed before needing to reapply additional paint.*

5 See Step 4. Using yellow and orange acrylic paints, follow Step 4 until stars and "Boo" are complete. Let paint dry for 30 minutes.

6 Using paint markers in matching colors, draw stitch marks along outside of any images you wish to define. *Use markers to add little stars or designs, and eyes, nose, and mouth to ghosts as desired.*

7 Beginning at one end of bucket handle, tie on longest fabric strip, wrapping it tightly around the whole handle. Tie at opposite end to secure.

8 Tie one fabric strip to each end of handle.

Harvest Basket

Weaving baskets is one of the oldest crafts in the world, dating back thousands of years. You can make this handsome centerpiece by weaving strips of fabric through a loosely woven basket.

What You Need

Coordinating cotton fabrics:
    2–5 different patterns
    (1 yd. each)

Fabric scissors

Loosely woven basket

Ruler

What to Do

1 Measure in 1" from one end of fabric. Using fabric scissors, make small cut. Tear fabric into 1"-wide strip.

2 Weave fabric strip through reeds of basket, down one side, across bottom, and up opposite side to make certain that 1 yd. is enough length. Length of strips will vary, depending on size of basket. Tie two strips together if necessary to finish a row.

Step 2

3 Repeat Step 1 for each fabric as needed.

Completed Harvest Basket

4 Knot each strip to top reed, leaving 1" tail. Weave each strip through basket. Change fabrics to create desired pattern. Keep weaving until all reeds of basket are entirely woven with fabric strips.

Harvest Tablecloth & Napkins

Cultures all over the world celebrate bountiful harvests. Help make your family's celebration more festive by using real fruits and vegetables to decorate the tablecloth and napkins.

What You Need

Cutting board
Fabric paints: assorted
Fruits: assorted
Kitchen knife
Permanent pens: assorted
Sponge brush
Tablecloth and napkins: light-colored
Vegetables: assorted

What You Need

Stamping Tips:

• Use the same fruits and vegetables to make many prints. Because mushrooms are very absorbent and soft, they will need to be replaced after every five prints.

• Do not use watery vegetables like tomatoes. They do not make good prints.

• Be aware that intensely colored juices from certain fruits and vegetables (like cherries or beets) will mix with paint and change color.

• Cover clothes with smock or old shirt. Fabric paints are permanent.

• Use permanent pen for adding details, like apple seeds.

• Instead of buying fabric paints, try adding fabric medium to acrylic paints, following manufacturer's instructions. The paints stay permanent.

What To Do

1 Cut fruits and vegetables in half lengthwise on cutting board.

2 Place tablecloth on <u>uncarpeted floor</u>. A little fabric paint may go through tablecloth onto floor. It can be wiped up easily from any nonporous surface like tile or linoleum. Fabric paint will stain carpet.

3 Using sponge brush, apply paint(s) onto cut side of fruit or vegetable.

4 Start from center of tablecloth and work out. Place paint side down and walk your fingers along the entire fruit or vegetable half, making certain paint is transferred onto tablecloth. Lift fruit or vegetable straight off.

Step 3

5 Add more paint and continue to print. Change fruit or vegetable as desired.

6 Fill tablecloth with fruit and vegetable prints as desired. Let dry for one hour.

7 Repeat Steps 3–5 with single fruit or vegetable on each napkin.

Step 4

Check This Out: Fruit and vegetable printing works well on paper. Use heavy-weight paper to print invitations, place cards, or paper napkin rings. You are now all set for a great family feast. Enjoy!

Christmas Decoupage Plates

Serve Santa cookies on these fun plates that showcase your artwork. Make one each year and watch how your art changes over time.

What You Need

What You Need

Clear glass plates

Craft scissors

Crayons or colored pencils

Decoupage glue

Pencil

Sponge brushes (2)

Tissue paper: blue; green; red

White acrylic paint

White drawing paper or
computer paper: 8½" x 11"

Wide-mouth aluminum can

What to Do

1 Place plate on sheet of white paper. Using pencil, trace around base (bottom) of plate. Remove plate.

2 Using crayons or colored pencils, draw a holiday scene inside traced area. Fill up space with color. For multiple gift plates, make photocopies of drawing or make several drawings. Cut out scene along traced line.

3 Place plate upside down on can. Using sponge brush, paint back base of plate with decoupage glue.

4 Press drawing face down on base of plate. Using your fingers, smooth out any air bubbles.

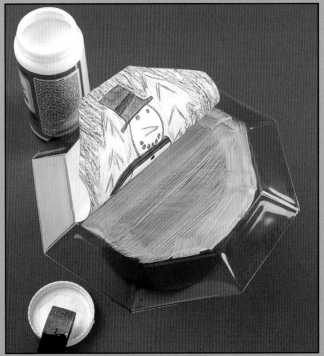

Step 4

5 Tear tissue paper into small pieces. Using sponge brush, paint back rim of plate with decoupage glue.

6 Press torn pieces of tissue paper onto back rim of plate. Be sure to overlap pieces of tissue paper, covering the whole rim. *Don't worry if some pieces hang over edges of rim. These will be trimmed later.* Let plate dry for one hour.

7 Trim away extra paper from edges of rim.

8 Using remaining sponge brush, paint back of plate with white paint. Let dry for several hours.

9 Wash decorative plates with a damp sponge only. Do not put them in dishwasher.

A glass platter can be used for this project. The decorative border on this platter was made by punching out small trees from decorative paper with a specialty punch. Trees were glued onto back of platter's rim, then tissue paper was glued behind them. Use this technique or create your own variation for your plate or platter.

Christmas Decoupage Frame

Relive wonderful Christmas memories with a picture frame designed by you from recycled wrapping paper, featuring a photo that captures the joy and excitement of Christmas morning. Decoupage glue adheres and seals the wrapping paper and provides a glossy finish, making this a quick and easy project.

52

What You Need

What You Need

Christmas wrapping papers
  (5–8 varieties)
Craft scissors
Decoupage glue: glossy finish
Picture frame
Sponge brush

What to Do

1 Tear wrapping paper into small, odd-shaped pieces.

2 Using sponge brush, paint decoupage glue on outside of frame.

3 Press torn paper pieces on decoupaged area of frame. Be sure to overlap paper pieces. Using your fingers, smooth out any air bubbles. Don't worry if some pieces hang over edges of frame. These will be trimmed later. Keep decorating and papering until the whole frame is covered.

Step 3

4 Paint decoupage glue on frame to seal papers. Let frame dry for several hours.

5 Trim away extra paper from edges of frame.

Check This Out: The word decoupage comes from the French word, "decouper", which means "to cut out." Decoupage traces its history back to the Middle Ages. For centuries, people have enjoyed cutting out decorative papers and gluing them to furniture, walls, boxes, and other surfaces. Even the famous French courtier, Marie Antoinette, enjoyed making decoupage projects!

Instead of the frame, try decorating the cardboard insert that fits inside. This will make a colorful and festive mat for your holiday photograph!

Paper Bag Tree Ornaments

Transform a simple brown paper grocery bag, into keep-sake ornaments to be enjoyed for many years to come simply by adding paint, polyester filling, ribbons, and raffia.

What You Need (for one)

Acrylic paints: black; green; orange; red; white

Black permanent marker

Brown paper grocery bag

Cotton Christmas fabric: ½"-square (2)

Craft glue

Hole punch: ⅛"

Paintbrushes: liner; flat, ¾"-wide

Pencil

Polyester filling: thin

Raffia (32")

Red and green striped ribbon (8")

Scissors: craft; pinking

Small red buttons

Spring operated clothespins

Twine (10")

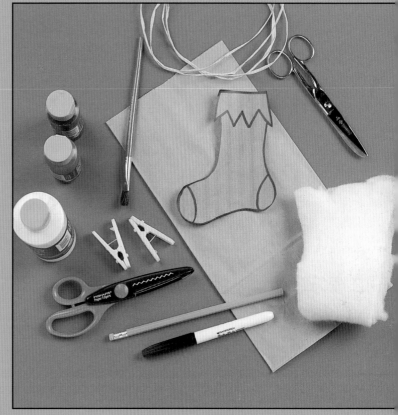

What You Need

What to Do

1 Using craft scissors, cut sides of grocery bag so that top and bottom pieces lie flat on top of each other.

2 Using pencil, draw shape of desired ornament onto brown paper bag. Bell, star, Santa, or Christmas tree are some ideas you can use for your ornament.

3 Using craft scissors, cut out drawn ornament shape from two layers of grocery bag, leaving ½" border around edge.

4 Using flat paintbrush, paint outside of each ornament shape.

55

5 Dip pencil eraser into white paint. Press eraser down on ornament shape, making sure dots are solid. Redip eraser into paint and press as necessary. Let dry for 30 minutes.

6 Using liner brush, make stripes. Let dry for 30 minutes.

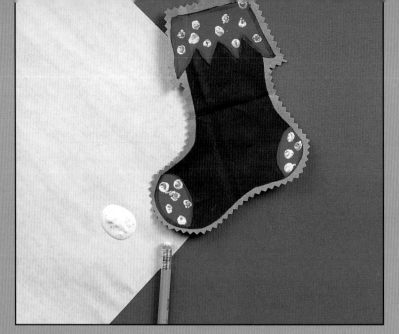

Step 5

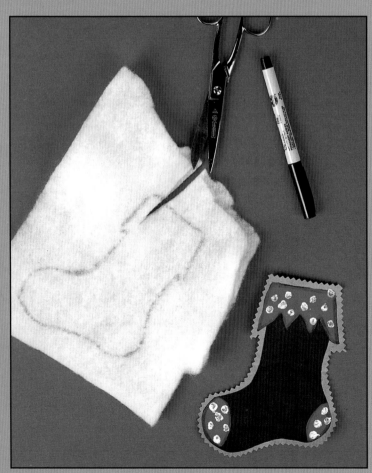

Step 9

7 Using marker, draw small stitch marks along painted edge of ornament shape.

8 Hold two identical ornament shapes together. Using pinking scissors, trim outside of ornament shape, leaving ¼" of border around painted edges.

9 Using marker, trace shape onto doubled polyester filling. Remove ornament. Using craft scissors, cut out layers of polyester filling ½" inside of drawn outline.

10 Place one half of ornament face down on work surface. Glue both layers of polyester filling onto ornament half. Run a small line of glue along inside edge.

11 Press remaining half of ornament on glue line. Pinch edges together with your fingers. Using clothespins, clamp edges together. Let dry for one hour. Remove clothespins.

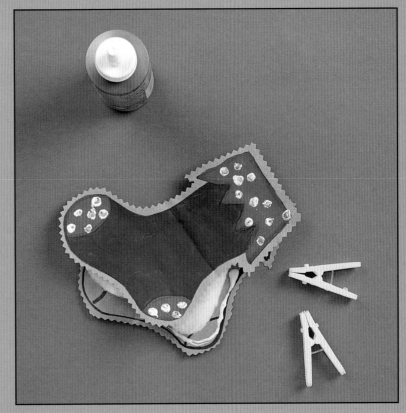

Steps 10–11

12 Using hole punch, punch one hole in each top corner of ornament. Insert ends of twine through holes. Knot to secure.

13 Glue small buttons, fabric squares, and ribbons onto ornament as desired.

14 Cut raffia into 8" pieces. Tie raffia strands onto twine on one side of ornament.

Holiday Photo Box

Decorative papers and paper punches turn any old box into a holiday photo box. Store photographs from this year's celebration as well as previous years'. When you and your family look through them, you will relive the fun and festivities.

What You Need

What You Need

Box with lid

Decorative-edged scissors: assorted

Glue: craft; glue stick

Paper punches: assorted holiday themes

Paper trimmer

Permanent marker

Scrapbook papers: assorted patterns; assorted solid colors

Ruler

What to Do

1 See **Measuring Boxes** on page 15. Measure lid and around all four sides of box. Using paper trimmer, cut pieces of solid paper ½"–1" smaller than dimensions of lid and vertical measurement of box.

2 Using decorative-edged scissors, trim edges of cut paper.

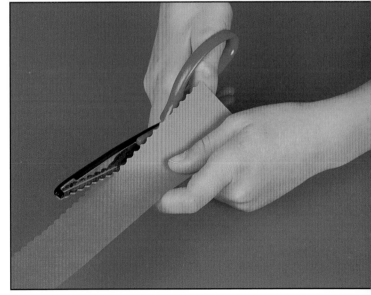

Step 2

3 Using glue stick, glue paper pieces onto box.

4 Using decorative-edged scissors, cut narrow strips of coordinating paper. Glue papers onto box as desired.

5 Using paper punches, punch out a variety of shapes from patterned scrapbook paper.

Step 5

If box has a hinged lid, make a small ribbon handle for easier opening. Fold a piece of 5" ribbon in half. Using craft glue, glue ends inside center of lid 1" from edge. Let dry, leaving lid open to prevent lid from being glued shut.

6 Using glue stick, glue shapes onto lid and sides of box as desired.

7 Using marker, write "Christmas Photos" or desired title on a piece of solid paper.

8 Using paper trimmer and decorative-edged scissors, trim box title.

9 Using glue stick, glue title onto center of box lid.

Room Stuff

Bedroom Sign

Let the world know who lives in your room by crafting this sign for your door. Choose rubber stamp images that express who you are. Stamp messages to your visitors with a small rubber stamp alphabet set.

What You Need

What You Need

Acrylic sealer

Adhesive-backed wooden letters (to spell out your name and the word "room")

Black permanent ink pad

Black permanent marker

Colored pencils

Hammer

Nails

Paper towels

Red acrylic paint

Rubber stamps: assorted

Sandpaper: medium-grit

Sawtooth picture hanger

Sponge brushes (2)

Spray polyurethane

Wooden sign board

What to Do

1 Sand sign board until smooth. Using damp paper towel, wipe off sign board.

2 Using sponge brush, seal sign board with acrylic sealer, following manufacturer's instructions. Let dry for several hours.

3 Using other sponge brush, paint letters with red acrylic paint. Let dry for one hour.

4 Peel protective paper off back of letters, revealing adhesive. Place letters on sign board as desired. Using marker, add punctuation, if necessary.

5 See **Rubber Stamping** on page 16. Ink and print each stamp onto sign board as desired. Let dry overnight.

Step 5

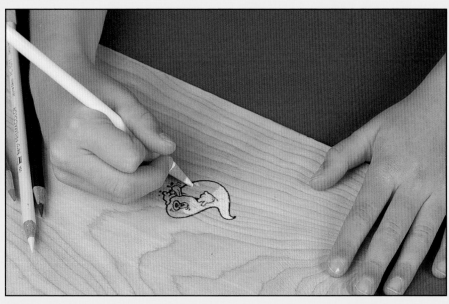

6 Using colored pencils, color in images.

Step 6

7 Spray several coats of polyurethane onto sign board, following manufacturer's instructions.

8 Using hammer and nails, attach sawtooth hanger to top center back of sign board.

Glittery Jewelry Holder

Wow! Being organized has never been prettier. This glittery jewelry holder will keep your necklaces, bracelets, and earrings neatly on display, making it a snap to get dressed each morning.

What You Need

What to Do

1 Sand picture frame, making it smooth.

2 Using sponge brush, paint the whole frame with blue paint. Let dry for 30 minutes. Add a second coat, if necessary. Let second coat dry for 30 minutes.

3 Using other sponge brush, paint all wooden stars with pink paint. While paint is still wet, lightly sprinkle on pink glitter. Shake off extra. Let dry for 15 minutes.

What You Need

Acrylic paints: blue; pink

Black permanent marker

Craft glue

Craft scissors

Disposable paintbrush

Earring backs

Fine-grit sandpaper

Flat-head tacks

Glitter: pink; silver

Plastic canvas

Rhinestones: pink; blue

Silver picture-hanging hooks (3)

Sponge brushes (2)

Star stencil

Wooden picture frame

4 Place star stencil on frame. Using paintbrush, apply a thin layer of glue inside star stencil. Remove stencil and lightly sprinkle silver glitter onto glue. Shake off extra. Let dry for 15 minutes.

Step 4

5 Using marker, line silver star with little, broken stitch lines.

6 Apply craft glue on backs of all but three small stars and place onto frame. Apply craft glue on back of rhinestones. Place onto frame as desired.

7 Trim plastic canvas so that it fits on back of frame. Glue plastic canvas onto frame.

Step 7

8 Glue front, flat portion of each picture hook onto backs of remaining pink stars.

9 Push tack through hole in each picture hook and through plastic canvas. Secure picture hooks to plastic canvas with earring backs.

10 Hang necklaces and bracelets from star hooks. Attach pierced earrings directly through plastic canvas.

Treasure Mirror

Craft sticks

Disposable
   mixing cup

Junk treasures

Latex gloves

Masking tape

Measuring
   spoons

Mirror with frame:
   plain wood
   or plaster

Plaster of paris

Sponge brush

Water

White acrylic
   paint

Do you have a special collection of treasures you have saved from goodie bags, swaps with friends, fast food restaurants, and gumball machines? Display them for everyone to see on this jazzy mirror. Every time you look in the mirror, you'll also be looking back at all the fun times you had collecting your treasures.

What to Do

1 Remove mirror from frame, if possible. If not, place strips of masking tape on mirror where mirror and frame meet. This will keep the mirror clean while you paint and plaster the frame.

2 Using sponge brush, paint frame.

💜 **3** Wearing latex gloves and using craft stick, mix six tablespoons of plaster of paris with two tablespoons of water in mixing cup.

💜 **4** Using craft stick, apply ½"-thick layer of plaster of paris mixture along one side of frame. Try to avoid getting plaster of paris on edges of frame.

5 Push variety of treasures deep into plaster of paris mixture. Cover most of surface area. Try filling small areas with beads.

6 Repeat Steps 4–5 on remaining sides of frame.

Steps 4–5

7 Let frame dry for three hours. Replace mirror or remove masking tape.

Check This Out: If you need more objects to complete this project, go on a treasure hunt for old puzzle pieces, old game pieces, old buttons, bottle caps, beads, nuts and bolts, decorative erasers, and doll shoes to name just a few.

Sports Clock

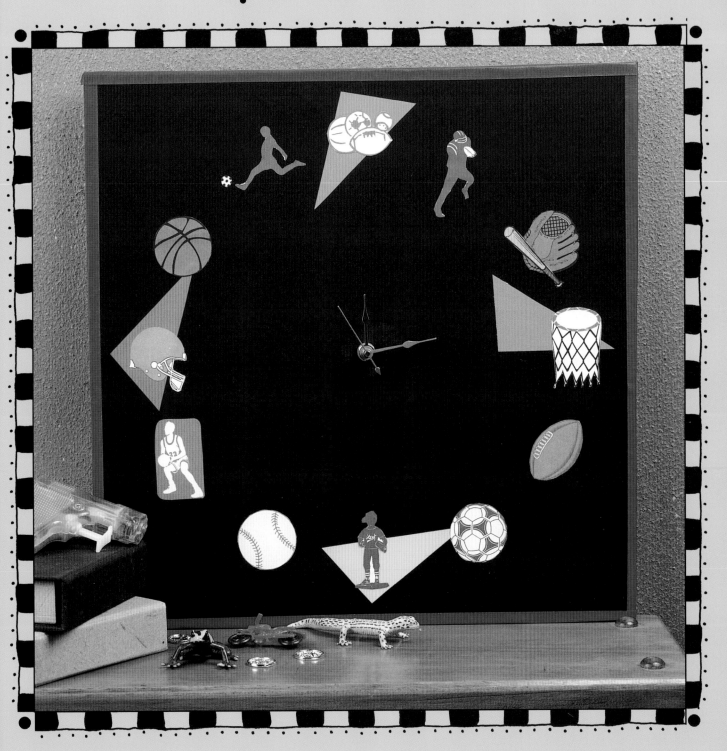

Your favorite sports decorate this clock, which is easy to make and fun to use.

What You Need

Awl

Black foam-core board: 14"-square

Blue masking tape

Clock workings kit

Color copies of 12 sports images:
 2"-square (reduce or enlarge as
 needed) (1 each)

Craft scissors

Glue stick

Paper scraps: blue; bright green;
 yellow; red

Pencil

Yardstick

Check This Out: The first clock was a sundial, invented by the Egyptians in 8000 B.C. About 600 years later, the Egyptians began dividing days into 24 hours. They used their clocks to help determine their planting schedule. Clocks evolved over time into water clocks, pendulum clocks, cuckoo clocks, electrical clocks, and digital clocks. It will be fun to watch how this familiar machine continues to evolve in the new millennium.

What to Do

1 Place yardstick from one corner of foam-core board to opposite diagonal corner. Using pencil, mark half way point. *This will be center back of clock.*

2 Press awl through foam-core board at center point.

Step 2

3 Place tape along each edge of foam-core board, over-lapping front of board ¼". Flatten tape around edges and back of foam-core board. Trim off extra tape at corners.

4 Cut out color copies of sports images. Cut out four irregularly shaped triangles from each color of scrap paper.

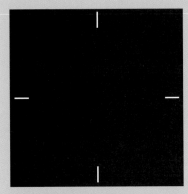

Diagram A

5 Measure and mark each side of foam-core board 7" from either corner, creating center placement for numbers on each side. See **Diagram A**. Apply glue on backs of triangles. Place directly over pencil marks where 12:00, 3:00, 6:00, and 9:00 would be.

Diagram B

6 See **Diagram B**. Mark points where remaining clock numbers would appear.

7 Apply glue on backs of each sports image. Place where numbers would be on clock. Make certain 1:00 and 11:00, 2:00 and 10:00, 3:00 and 9:00, 4:00 and 8:00, 5:00 and 7:00, and 6:00 and 12:00 are even with each other.

8 Insert clock kit at center point of clock, following manu-facturer's instructions.

Wear It
Polar Fleece Scarf & Hat

Chase away those winter blues with a cheerful hat and scarf made from polar fleece. You are the designer. Pick fabric and ribbons to coordinate with your coat. With only one seam to sew (or glue), this set is easy to make. Best of all, it will keep you fashionably warm and toasty all winter long.

What You Need

Buttons: 1"-dia., yellow (9)

Coordinating thread

Craft stick

Fabric glue

Fabric scissors

Needle

Red polar fleece: 60"-wide
(1 yd.)

Rubber band

Straight pins

Tape measure

Yellow floral rickrack: med.
(2⅓ yds.)

Yellow grosgrain ribbon:
½"-wide (1⅓ yds.)

What You Need

What To Do

1 Cut off **Selvage Edges** from polar fleece. Discard edges.

Selvage Edges—rough edges that have small perforations.

Scarf

2 Measure and cut 9" x 60" piece of polar fleece. Measure and cut rickrack into four 9" pieces. Measure and cut two 9" pieces of ribbon.

3 See **Diagram A**. Using craft stick, apply fabric glue on back of rickrack and ribbons. Place them onto end of scarf. Repeat for other end of scarf.

4 Cut both ends of fleece into strips of fringe 3" x ½".

5 Sew or glue three evenly spaced **Buttons** onto each piece of ribbon. If glued, let dry for two hours.

Diagram A

Button

1. Thread needle. Knot ends together. Place button right side up on fabric where desired.

2. Insert needle up through fabric and first button hole. Go down through second button hole and fabric. Do this six times or until button feels secure.

3. Insert needle through thread on bottom, creating loop. Insert needle through loop, knotting to secure. Trim off extra thread.

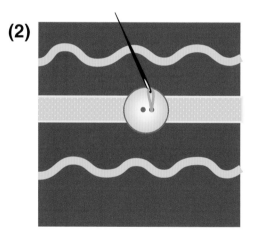

(2)

Hat

1 Measure and cut one 18" x 22" piece of fleece. Measure and cut one 22" piece of ribbon and two 22" pieces of rickrack.

2 Place fleece on work surface with 22" sides at top and bottom.

3 Measure, fold up, and pin 2½" cuff from bottom of fleece.

4 Using craft stick, apply fabric glue onto the back of cut ribbon and rickrack. Place onto hat. See photo at right. Let glue dry for two hours.

Step 4

5 Sew **Buttons** onto ribbon as desired.

6 Fold fleece lengthwise, with right sides together. Be sure ends of rickrack and ribbon are lined up at seam. Pin sides together. **See Diagram B**.

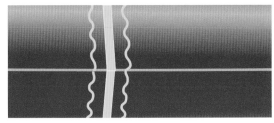

Diagram B

7 **Whipstitch** or glue seam closed. Remove pins. If glued, let dry for two hours. Turn hat right side out.

Whipstitch

1. Bring needle up at A; taking a small stitch. Slide needle through folded edge of fabric about ⅛" to ¼" and out at B.

2. Repeat until seam is closed.

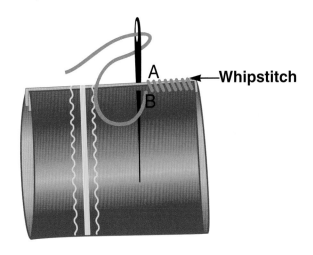

75

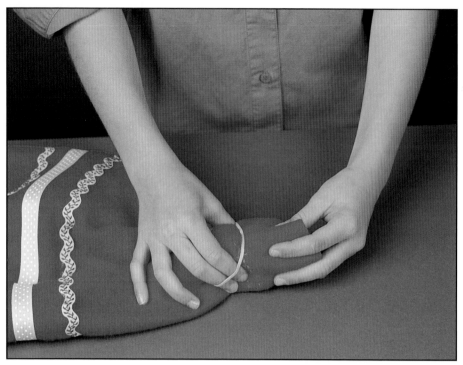

Step 8

8 Gather top of hat in hand and wrap rubber band around fabric, placing it 5" down from top.

9 Cut 1" x 8" strip from extra polar fleece. Wrap and tie strip over rubber band.

10 Cut top of hat into 3½" x ½" strips of fringe.

Check This Out:
Polar fleece is made by melting recycled plastic bottles. Now that is inventive recycling!

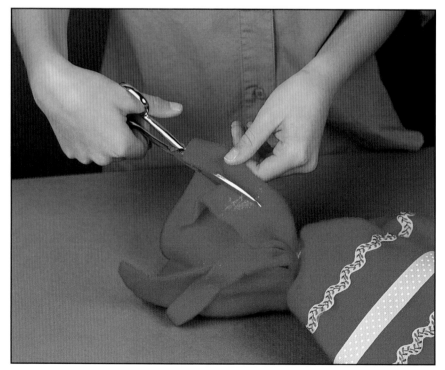

Step 10

Denim Jacket with Patches

Turn an ordinary denim jacket into something special. Bits of felt and glue are all you need to make a complete transformation.

What You Need

What to Do

1 Using pencil, draw shapes for patches on nonwaxy side of freezer wrap.

2 Using craft scissors, loosely cut around shapes. *They will be cut out more carefully later.*

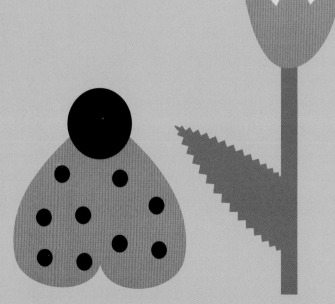

Ideas for Shapes

78

3 Preheat iron on medium-high setting. Place freezer wrap shapes, waxy side down, on desired felt scrap. Iron freezer wrap onto felt—it takes about 10 seconds to stick.

4 Using fabric scissors or pinking scissors, cut out shape along pencil outline. *You've just created a patch.* Peel off freezer wrap.

Step 4

5 Decorate patch with details cut from felt, such as eyes, wings, etc. Using fabric glue and toothpick, glue details onto patch.

6 Make felt patches stand out by adding layers of colors and ribbons of felt on top of each other. See **Creating Patches** on page 80.

Idea for Shape

7 Glue completed patch onto denim jacket as desired.

Creating Patches

1. Draw butterfly shape on freezer wrap. Iron shape onto pink felt scrap.

2. Using fabric scissors, cut around shape along pencil outline. Peel off freezer wrap. Repeating process with the same piece of freezer wrap, cut out upper part of wings from blue felt and body section from yellow felt.

3. Layer pieces over matching parts.

4. Using fabric glue and toothpick, glue pieces in place. Decorate butterfly with orange stripes and multicolor spirals. See **Creating Felt Spirals**.

Ideas for Shapes

Creating Felt Spirals

1. Cut ¼"-wide strips of two contrasting colors of felt. Lay one on top of the other and tightly roll up to 1" from end. Trim inside piece ½" shorter than outside piece.

2. Using toothpick, apply fabric glue on top of exposed ends of both strips of felt. Keep rolling until completely coiled. Press ends down so coil does not unravel when glue dries.

Creating Felt Spirals: Step 2

Sunflower Beach Bag & Hat

Head for the beach with this adorable beach bag and hat you've designed yourself. All it takes is a few minutes and some ribbon, silk flowers, and glue. You will be all set for a fashionable day in the sun.

What You Need

Craft glue

Craft stick

Green thread

Grosgrain ribbons:
    ½"-wide, green polka-dot (12")
    ⅞"-wide, green polka-dot (9")
    1"-wide, green (14")

Needle

Ribbon bumblebee and ladybug

Scissors: craft; fabric

Silk flowers (4)

Straw bag

Yellow baseball hat

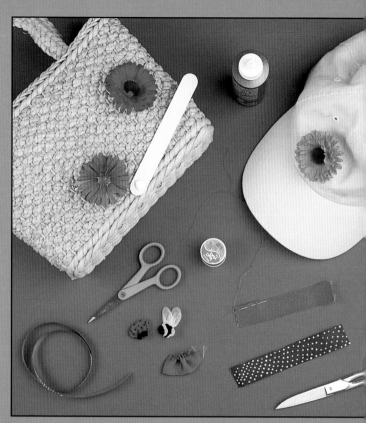

What You Need

What to Do

1 Using craft stick, apply glue on back of silk flowers. *If flowers still have stems, use craft scissors to cut them off.* Place on straw bag as desired, pressing down for one minute.

2 Cut 1"-wide ribbon into three equal lengths.

3 Make three **Gathered Leaves.**

Gathered Leaf

1. Thread and knot needle with thread. Fold ribbon in half, matching short ends. Gather-stitch along one edge.

2. Pull thread to gather. Knot to secure. Trim off extra thread. Turn sewn ribbon inside out.

3. Shape leaf.

(1)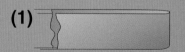

(2)

(3)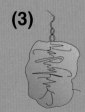

82

4 Using craft stick, apply glue on back of leaves. Place on bag, laying them crossways to stem you will place later, pressing down for one minute.

5 Using fabric scissors, cut ½"-wide ribbon into three equal lengths.

6 Glue stem onto bag, placing one end under flower and one edge over beginning of leaf.

7 Using craft stick, apply glue on back of bumblebee. Place onto bag as desired, pressing down for one minute.

8 Let bag dry for two hours.

Hat

1 Cut ⅞"-wide ribbon in half. Create two **Gathered Leaves**. See page 82.

2 Using craft stick, apply glue on back of flower and leaves. Place onto center of hat. Apply glue on back of ladybug. Place above flower. Let dry for two hours.

Completed Hat

Check This Out: How about throwing a "School's Out for the Summer Party!" Let each guest decorate their own beach bag and hat. Straw bags and baseball hats can be bought very inexpensively at discount stores. Check at your local craft store for bags of silk flowers that have missing stems.

These flowers are inexpensive since the heads have limited application. Supply a variety of ribbons and glue and let your friends create all afternoon. Each time they pull out their beautiful beach bag and hat, they will remember the wonderful afternoon spent with you.

Doodle-art Footwear

What You Need

Permanent paint pens:
   assorted colors

Rubber flip-flops: sized to fit

Doodle to your heart's content with permanent paint pens and turn ordinary flip-flops into great footwear for a trip to the beach. Silk flowers can be added using cement glue.

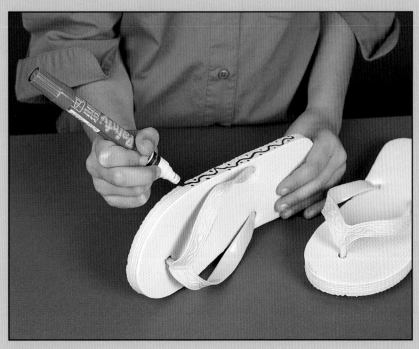

Step 1

What to Do

1 Shake pens, following manufacturer's instructions. Doodle on flip-flops with one pen as desired. Let paint dry for five minutes.

2 Doodle on flip-flops with another color pen. Keep doodling as desired. Let each color dry for five minutes before starting a new color.

3 Let flip-flops dry for 15 minutes before wearing.

Trips
Travel Board Game

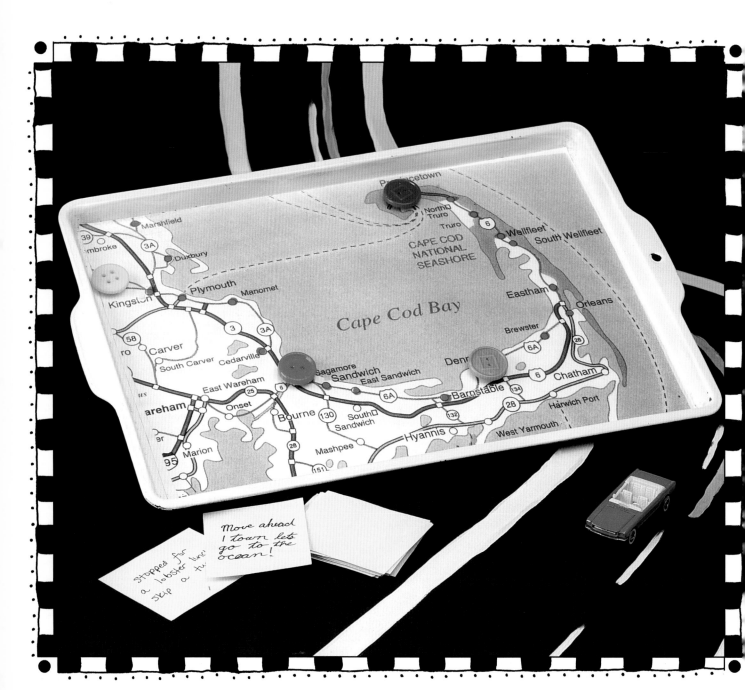

You won't notice how long the car trip is on your next vacation because you will be too busy playing this board game that you made yourself with the map of your route. The playing pieces are magnetic so that bumps in the road won't spoil your fun.

What You Need

What You Need

Baking sheet (spray-painted if desired)

Buttons: assorted colors (4)

Clear cement glue

Color copy machine with enlargement capability

Double-sided tape

Index cards

Map of travel route

Pencil

Red permanent marker

What to Do

1 Using copy machine, enlarge map showing travel route to fit inside baking sheet.

2 Using marker, highlight towns that you will be passing through.

3 Using double-sided tape, attach map to baking sheet

4 Using clear cement glue, glue magnets to back of buttons. *You've just created game pieces.* Let dry for three hours.

5 Using pencil and index cards, create **Chance Cards** for game.

6 Play game. Keep chance cards face down on board. Each player selects a game piece and takes a turn drawing chance cards. Follow route through each town until destination is reached. The first one there wins.

Step 4

Chance cards — tell each player what to do or how many spaces to advance or move back. Match chance cards with events that may occur on your trip. Examples for an east coast vacation might include: stopped for a lobster dinner, skip a turn; or hurry to the beach for a swim, move ahead three spaces. Examples for a mountain vacation might include: Eeeks!—there's a bear in the road, go back to the previous town; stop to build a campsite, skip a turn. Writing chance cards is a lot of fun. You may want to save it as a traveling activity.

You are lost! Go back to the beginning and start over!

Travel Craft Kit

Whether going hundreds of miles or just across town, traveling is more fun when you have your portable arts and crafts kit with you. This handy box stores all your favorite craft supplies. Add pockets to help you stay organized. You may also use the box as your work surface.

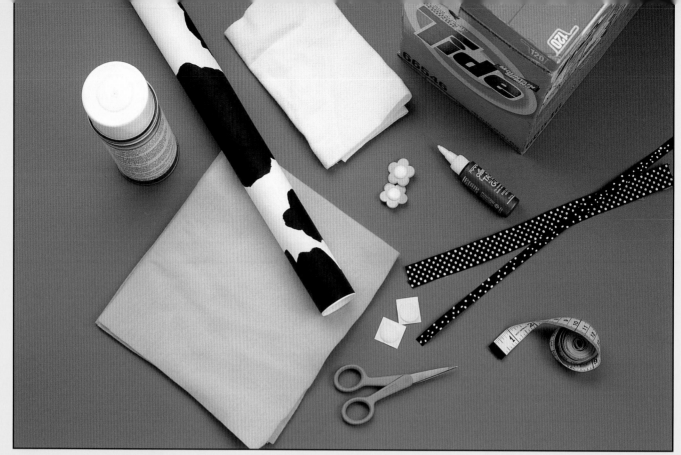

What You Need

What You Need

Adhesive-backed paper (1 yd.)

Cloth

Craft glue

Craft scissors

Decorative buttons (6)

Felt (6 squares)

Detergent box with handle: large, empty

Ribbons: ¾"-wide (48")
  ¼"-wide (2 yds.)

Tape measure

Velcro® closures (3)

White spray paint

What to Do

1 Thoroughly clean out box with damp cloth.

2 In a well-ventilated area, spray-paint inside and outside of box. Let dry for two hours.

3 See **Measuring Boxes** on page 15. Measure outside of box lid, including overhanging lip. Using those dimensions, cut a piece of adhesive-backed paper to size.

4 Measure four sides of box. Using those dimensions, cut a piece of adhesive-backed paper to size.

5 Peel off lining from back of paper for box lid. Place center of paper onto center of box lid. Using your fingers, smooth paper over entire box lid, pressing out any air bubbles.

6 Make small cuts in paper at corner of overhanging lip. Using your fingers, smooth paper down onto lip. Trim away extra paper from corners and edges of lip.

7 Peel off lining from back of paper for sides of box. Place center of paper onto center of box front. Using your fingers, smooth paper over all four sides, pressing out any air bubbles.

8 Trim away extra paper from edges of box.

9 Measure and cut ¾"-wide ribbon to cover overhanging lip of box. Glue ribbon onto lip of box. Glue five evenly spaced buttons onto ribbon.

Step 9

Envelope-shaped Pockets

10 Measure inside of box lid. Using those dimensions, cut piece of felt to size.

11 Cut another piece of felt to same width and add 3" to length.

12 Place smaller felt piece onto larger felt piece, aligning them along bottom. Glue bottom and sides of smaller felt piece onto larger felt piece. *You've created a pocket with flap.*

13 Cut edges of pocket flap to taper them.

Step 13

14 Glue loop part of Velcro® onto inside center of pocket flap. Fold down flap to align Velcro pieces. Glue hook part of Velcro® onto pocket.

15 Measure edges of pocket flap and three sides of pocket. Using those dimensions, cut six pieces of ¼"-wide ribbon. Glue ribbon pieces onto edges of pocket flap and pocket sides. Glue completed pocket onto inside of box lid.

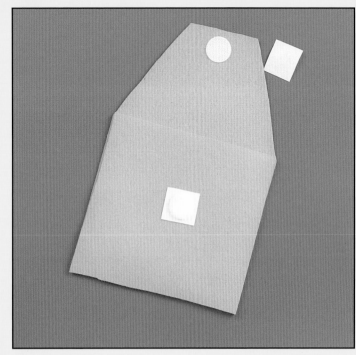

Step 14

16 Decide how large you would like outside pockets. Cut felt to size.

17 See Steps 11–15. Follow steps until outside pockets are completed.

18 Glue one button onto flap of one outside pocket.

There are many wonderful craft supplies that aren't too messy to take on the road. Pack your box with colored and patterned papers, stickers, glue stick, blunt-tipped scissors, rubber stamps, markers (glue marker box to the inside of travel kit), ruler, pipe cleaners, beading materials, tape, small white bags (great for making puppets), stencils, and anything else you can think of. Throw in some wet naps or baby wipes to clean up messy fingers. Don't use the supplies in your travel kit for home projects. This way the travel kit will always be ready to go whenever you are.

"Make a Statement" Photo Mat

What You Need

Cardboard photo mat
Craft scissors
Glue stick
Magazines
Newspapers
Photograph
Picture frame

When traveling with your family, take along some old magazines and newspapers that you have permission to use. As you travel, cut out words that express your feelings about your trip, vacations, family, exploring, and your specific destination. Glue these words to a photo mat and then finish off the frame with a favorite picture from your vacation, creating a wonderful keepsake.

What to Do

1 Cut out words from newspapers and magazines. *You will need to cut a lot of words to cover the photo mat.*

2 Apply glue to back of words. Place words randomly onto photo mat. Vary size, color, and font of words. If part of word hangs over edge of photo mat, trim off extra. Let dry for one hour.

3 Place mat and photograph into frame.

Step 1

Check This Out: You can secretly make an extra photo mat and framed photograph to give your parents as a surprise, thanking them for the vacation with a wonderful memory of your trip.

Shadow Box Memories

What You Need

Acrylic box frame

Colored card stock

Colored masking tape

Colored paper

Craft glue

Craft knife

Craft scissors

Craft stick

Cutting board

Foam-core board scraps

Ruler

Trip mementos (photos, tickets, maps, guides, small souvenirs, etc.)

What You Need

Don't stash all those souvenirs from a favorite trip in a shoe box or drawer. Put the items on display in this shadow box so that you and your family can enjoy the memories for years to come. This project is easy to make with an acrylic box frame and fun, too, because it allows you to relive those memories.

What to Do

♥ **1** Remove cardboard box from inside of acrylic box frame. Turn cardboard box so that wrong side is facing up. Stand and hanging hole should be facing you. Using craft knife and ruler, cut off back of box.

2 Gently pull apart corners of cardboard box, placing it flat on work surface. Choose paper to line inside of box, making certain to cover the whole surface.

Step 1

3 Apply glue to inside of box. Place paper over glue and press flat, smoothing out any air bubbles. Run your finger-nails over folds to be sure paper sticks in creases. Let dry for five minutes.

4 Fold up sides of box. Glue corners in place. Pinch corners together for three minutes while glue sets. Be sure lining paper is still flat. Using your fingers, smooth out any air bubbles.

5 Using craft scissors, trim away extra paper from edges of box. Apply decorative tape to edges of box. Using your fingers, smooth out any wrinkles.

6 See **Mementos Techniques** on page 99.

7 Glue mementos inside box as desired. Let dry for one hour. Replace acrylic cover over box.

Mementos Techniques

Shadow boxes have depth, allowing the use of dimensional items. It is also fun to "pop out" mementos, so that they appear to be floating over the background.

1. Using craft knife, cut foam-core board slightly smaller than item.

2. Using craft stick, apply thin layer of glue to back of foam-core board. Place memento onto top of foam-core board.

3. Apply thin layer of glue to opposite side of foam-core board. Place onto lined box.

Mementos Techniques: Step 2

Paper mementos, such as photographs, tickets, and menus, look better layered onto colored card stock that has been cut slightly larger than paper item. The card stock frames your memento.

1. Glue paper memento onto colored card stock. Trim card stock ¼"–½" larger than paper memento.

If a paper memento is too large to fit into your frame, take it to a copy store and have it color copied and reduced to a size that works well for your project.

Use a map from your trip as background paper for your shadow box.

1. Glue map onto box, following Steps 2–5 on page 98.

Make labels identifying items in your shadow box. Include dates, places, and any interesting stories that you want to remember or that help explain the significance of the items in the shadow box.

Gifts
Collage Stationery

A few snips of paper, some rubber-stamped images, and colorful buttons—that's all you really need to make collage stationery.

What You Need

Brush art markers: assorted; black

Buttons: pink; yellow

Decorative papers: blue; orange; bright pink; white; white/black checkered; yellow

Glue: craft; glue stick

Purchased card and envelope pack

Rubber stamps: assorted

Ruler

Scissors: craft; pinking

What You Need

What to Do

1 See **Rubber Stamping** on page 16. Using black marker, ink stamp and print image onto white paper. Let ink dry for five minutes.

Step 1

2 Using colored markers, color in stamped image as desired.

3 Using craft or pinking scissors, cut out image, leaving ¼" border of white paper around image.

Step 2

4 Using craft and pinking scissors, cut out various shapes from decorative papers. Using glue stick, apply glue to backs of cut paper pieces and stamped images. Place onto card as desired.

5 Using craft glue, apply glue to backs of buttons. Place onto card as desired. Let dry for 30 minutes.

6 Using glue stick, apply glue on backs of cut paper pieces. Place onto envelope front as desired.

Check This Out:
In French, the word collage means "to glue." Create your own stationery by combining different materials that work together and gluing them onto your card—like leaves, acorns, natural-colored paper, printed paper that looks like animal skin, photos of animals, and raffia.

Collage Stationery Folder

After you have made the fun collage stationery shown on page 100, create this matching folder to keep it in. What a wonderful birthday gift this would make for a special friend!

What You Need

Brush art markers: black; assorted

Butter or table knife

Buttons: pink; yellow

Decorative papers: blue; orange; bright pink; white; white/black checkered; yellow

Glue: craft; glue stick

Pencil

Rubber stamps: assorted

Ruler

Scissors: craft; pinking

White poster board: 11½" x 9½"

What To Do

1 Place poster board on flat work surface with 11½" sides at top and bottom. Using pencil and ruler, measure and mark center point (5¾") on top and bottom of poster board.

2 Lay ruler on poster board at marks and **Score**.

Step 2

Score — to gently run butter or table knife down poster board along ruler, making a smooth crease. Take care not to cut through the poster board.

3 Using pencil and ruler, measure and mark 2½" up from bottom on each side. See **Diagram A**.

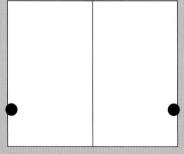

Diagram A

4 Lay ruler on poster board at marks and **Score**.

5 Fold poster board in along score lines. Fold in center, open, then fold up bottom. *You've just created a folder with one long flap pocket to insert stationery.*

6 Flatten folds. Using craft scissors, cut center sides of flap to score line. *Cut flap only, not folder.*

7 Using pencil and ruler, mark ½" on each side of cut made in Step 6. At bottom of folder, cut each side of flap in a diagonal to end of flap cut, making it easier to get stationery in and out. See **Diagram B**.

Step 8

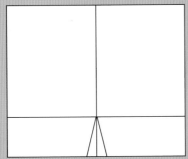

Diagram B

8 Fold up both sides of flap. Using glue stick, apply glue to outer edges of flap. Place folder under a heavy book, helping it to dry flat.

9 See **Rubber Stamping** on page 15. Using markers, ink stamp and print images onto decorative paper. Let ink dry for five minutes. Using colored markers, color in background of stamped image as desired.

10 Using craft or pinking scissors, cut out image. Cut out various shapes from decorative papers. Using glue stick, apply glue to backs of cut paper pieces, stamped images, and buttons. Place onto folder as desired.

11 Using black marker, create a title for folder on white paper. Using pinking scissors, cut out title. Using glue stick, apply glue to back of title. Place onto front of folder. Store stationery in folder.

Dimensions given for this project are meant to accommodate 4½" x 6" greeting cards and envelopes. If your cards are larger or smaller, adjust the dimensions accordingly.

Sunflower Pen

Beautiful handmade stationery deserves a special pen to go with it. You can make this one in minutes with colorful embroidery floss.

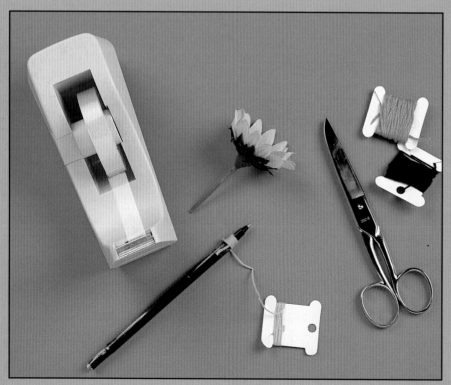

What You Need

What You Need

Craft glue

Craft scissors

Double-sided tape

Embroidery flosses: assorted colors (1 yd. of each color)

Pen without pocket clip

Silk flower with 2" stem

What to Do

1 Place double-sided tape along length of pen, leaving ½" near pen point uncovered.

2 Beginning at end of tape near pen point, place ¼" end of first color of floss lengthwise onto tape. Wind floss around pen widthwise, covering end of floss. Keep winding until stripe is as wide as desired.

3 Change colors of floss several times and keep winding floss around pen. When the whole pen, except 2" from top, has been covered, hold flower stem against pen and wind floss over both pen and stem, changing colors as desired.

4 When top of pen has been reached, trim off extra floss. Apply tiny dot of glue onto end of floss. Using your fingers, smooth onto pen. Let dry for 15 minutes.

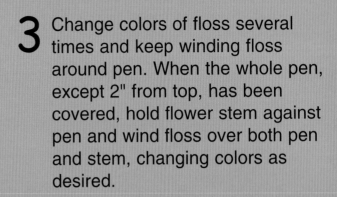

Ideas for Pen Top

Check This Out: Change the look of the pen by choosing different materials for wrapping. Try twine for a more rustic look or thin strips of paper wrapped on a diagonal for a very grown-up look. Satin ribbon would look beautiful too! Instead of topping the pen with a flower, consider topping your pen with a feather, curled wires, or a bouquet or ribbon flowers.

Decorative Candles

Collecting and displaying candles is so much fun, but it can be costly. By making your own candles, you'll have fun and save money, too.

What You Need (for one)

Flower-shaped cookie cutter: small

Hole punch: ¼"

Thin sheets of candle wax: assorted colors; black

White pillar candle

What to Do

1 Place one sheet of colored candle wax onto clean work surface.

2 Using cookie cutter, press cutter into wax. *You've just created a small flower.* Using your finger, press flower out of cookie cutter. Repeat for desired number of flowers. *Try a different shaped cookie cutter and design candle as desired.*

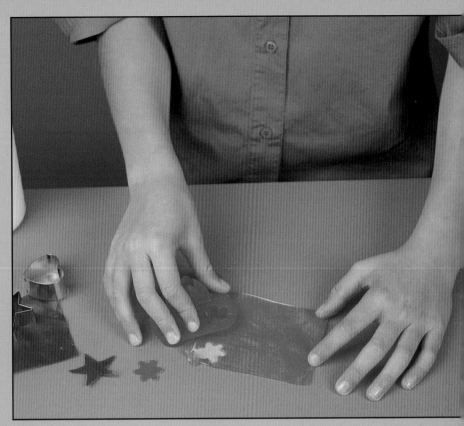

Step 2

Step 3

3 Using your fingers, press flowers onto candle. *Warmth from your fingers will make flowers stick to candle.*

4 Using hole punch, punch one small circle from black candle wax for each flower. Press circle into center of each flower.

Design-a-Stamp Gift Wrap

The first step in creating this cheerful gift wrap is to design and make your own rubber stamp. (It's so easy you will want to make a bunch.) Next, stamp cards, wrapping paper, gift bags, and tissue paper. Enjoy the delight your cheerful homemade wrapping brings to the lucky person receiving your gift.

What You Need

Acrylic paints: black; green; red

Aluminum foil

Black marker

Card stock: green; white

Clear acrylic candy boxes (2)

Craft foam

Double-sided tape

Fine-tipped green marker

Glue stick

Green polka-dot grosgrain ribbon: ½"-wide (1 yd.)

Hole punch

Pencil with eraser

Red/white checkered paper

Scissors: craft; decorative-edged

Sponge brush

White gift wrapping paper

What You Need

What to Do

Stamp

1 Using pencil, draw small cherry (without stem) and leaf separately on foam.

2 Using craft scissors, cut out cherry. Using decorative-edged scissors, cut out leaf. Using pencil, trace cherry and leaf onto other parts of foam.

3 Using craft scissors, cut out traced cherry. Using decorative-edged scissors, cut out traced leaf.

4 Using double-sided tape, attach ident-ical images toge-ther. *This layered foam will be called the "stamp." By building up the stamp with two layers, the printed image will be cleaner.*

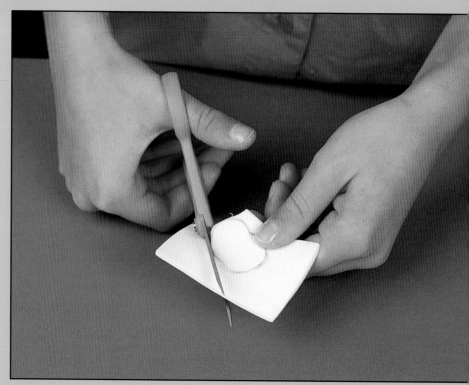

Step 3

5 For each stamp, place a piece of double-sided tape on center of candy box. Place stamp onto tape. *This will let you see where you're placing the image when printing.*

Wrapping Paper

6 Pour small amount of each paint color onto aluminum foil.

7 Dip corner of sponge into red paint. Ink cherry stamp with sponge by gently patting paint onto stamp until the whole stamp is covered. Place stamp onto white wrapping paper, pressing down lightly. Lift stamp straight off. Keep inking and printing as desired. Let dry for 15 minutes.

8 Using green marker, draw cherry stems onto wrapping paper.

9 Dip clean corner of sponge into green paint. Ink leaf stamp with sponge by gently patting paint onto stamp until the whole stamp is covered. Place stamp onto white wrapping paper at top of each stem, pressing down lightly. Lift stamp straight off. Keep inking and printing as desired. Let dry for 15 minutes.

Step 9 (A)

10 Dip pencil eraser into black paint. Press eraser on wrapping paper, making sure dots are solid. Redip eraser into paint and press as necessary. Let dry for 30 minutes.

Card

11 See Steps 6–9. Print two cherries and leaves onto white card stock. Draw cherry stems onto card. Let dry for 15 minutes.

12 Using black marker, print polka-dots onto white card stock.

13 Using decorative-edged scissors, trim card stock, leaving ½" border around printed images.

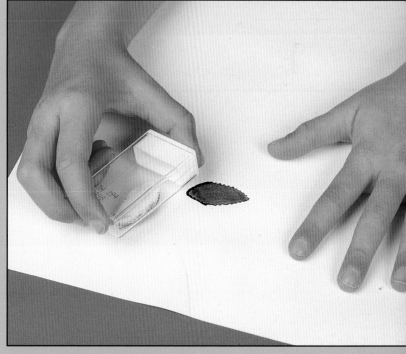

Step 9 (B)

113

14 Glue trimmed cherry card stock onto red and white checkered paper. Using decorative-edged scissors, trim paper, leaving ¾" border around card stock.

Completed Card

15 Glue checkered paper onto folded green card stock. *You've just created the card.*

16 Punch hole in upper left-hand corner of card. Thread 3" piece of ribbon through hole. Knot to secure.

Wrap your gift with this beautiful hand-made paper. Add the finishing touches by tying the gift with ribbon and tying the card to the ribbon.

Ideas for Stamps

Funky Recycled Candleholders

Mom and Dad will flip their lids for these wild candleholders made from metal jar lids and bottle caps. What a great gift for their anniversary!

What You Need

What You Need (for one)

Candlestick

Clear cement glue

Glass candleholder: 1"-high

Hammer

Jump rings: 12 mm (6)

Metal bottle caps (6)

Metal jar lids or canister lids: assorted sizes and colors (6–7)

Small glass jar or bud vase (no more than 3" high)

Small nail

What to Do

1 Stack three lids together. In a well-ventilated area, run a thin line of glue around rims of top two lids, forming candleholder base. Let dry overnight.

2 Glue jar or vase onto candleholder base. *Glue right side or wrong side up, whichever you prefer. Let dry overnight.*

Step 1

3 Using hammer and nail, make six evenly spaced holes around rim of largest remaining lid. Make one hole in center of each bottle cap.

4 Stack and glue remaining lids together. Be sure smallest lid is on top and largest lid with holes is on bottom. Let dry overnight.

5 Open jump ring, pulling one end toward you and pushing other end away from you. *Don't pull ends apart because this will weaken the jump ring, causing it to break.*

6 Thread jump ring through holes in bottle cap and lid. Close jump ring.

7 Repeat Steps 5–6 for remaining jump rings.

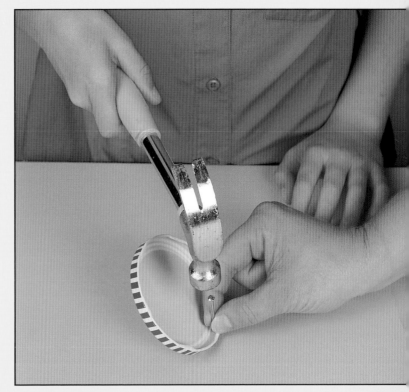

Step 3

8 Glue stack of lids onto top of jar or vase.

9 Glue glass candleholder onto top lid. Let dry overnight.

10 Place candlestick in candleholder.

Play Stuff

Snow People

These adorable dolls take no time to make, are fun to play with, and make great gifts. You may even clean out a few drawers, too! The dolls are made from knitted gloves, socks, and beans.

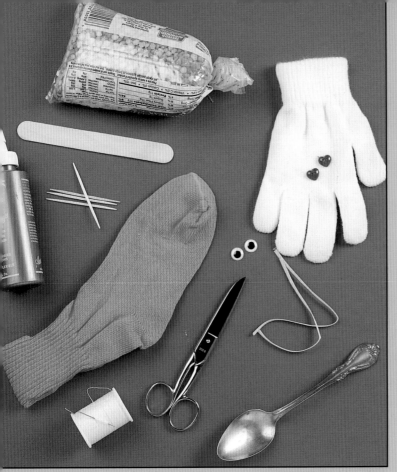

What You Need (for one)

Buttons (2)

Coordinating threads

Craft glue

Fabric scissors

Googly eyes (2)

Kitchen spoon

Knitted glove: child-sized (1)

Needle

Ribbed sock: child-sized (1)

Satin ribbon: ⅛"-wide (8")

Small dried beans

Toothpick

What You Need

What to Do

1 Fill bottom of glove with beans.

Step 1

2 Push thumb of glove to inside of glove. See **Diagram A**.

3 Continue to fill glove with beans, stopping 2" from top of glove. *It should be filled enough to have a shape, but should not be packed tightly.*

Diagram A

4 Cut ribbon in half. Tie one ribbon around glove, 2" from top. Tie other ribbon 2" below first ribbon. Trim off extra ribbon. *You've just created the head.*

5 Push 1" of each "arm" inside itself. This shortens the "arms", making them more like "people" arms.

6 Using needle and thread, **Whipstitch** ends of arms closed.

Whipstitch

1. Bring needle up at A; taking a small stitch. Slide needle through folded edge of fabric about ⅛" to ¼" and out at B.

2. Repeat until seam is closed.

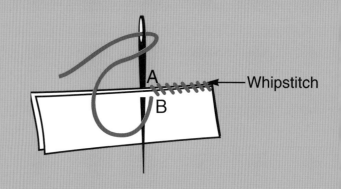

7 See **Diagram B**. Cut off foot area from sock, in front of heel. Roll up cut end of foot area twice, making 1½" cuff. *You've just created a hat.* (Toe will be at top of hat.) Place hat onto doll's head. Tack to secure, if desired.

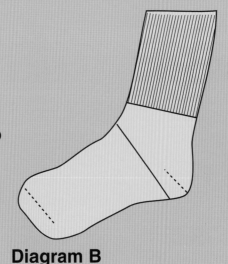

Diagram B

8 Cut off ribbing of sock, creating long tube. Cut two 1" pieces lengthwise from ribbing .

9 Using needle and coordinating thread, sew ribbing pieces together widthwise, creating one long piece of ribbing. *You've just created a scarf.* Tie scarf around doll's neck.

10 Using craft glue and toothpick or craft stick, apply glue on back of googly eyes and buttons. Place eyes and buttons onto doll. Let dry for 30 minutes.

Check This Out: Manufactured dolls became available in the late 1800's. Since many people could not afford to buy them, children would make their own dolls, as their parents and ancestors had done for hundreds of years before. These homemade dolls were much more affordable because they were made from materials found at home, like sawdust, beans, pieces of clothing, yarn, wood, wax, and even corn husks. These dolls are still less costly than manufactured ones. Their special beauty is that each one is unlike any other in the world because it is your own unique creation.

Baseball Card Box

What You Need

Acrylic paints: black; blue green; white

Color copies of seven baseball cards

Craft knife

Decoupage glue: matte finish

Old toothbrush

Paintbrush

Paper towels

Red permanent pen

Sponge brushes (2)

Wood glue

Wooden box with lid

Wooden knobs: 1½" (5)

What You Need

This cool box holds baseball cards or other collector cards in real style.

What to Do

1 Cut out color-copied baseball cards.

2 Using sponge brush, paint box with blue green acrylic paint. Using paper towels, wipe off some paint, giving box an aged, slightly worn look. Let box dry for 30 minutes.

3 Using paintbrush, paint wooden knobs with white paint. Let knobs dry for 30 minutes.

4 Using pen, draw stitch marks on wooden knobs. *You've just created baseballs.*

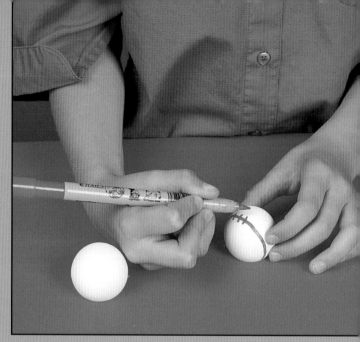

Step 4

5 Using other sponge brush, paint layer of decoupage glue on box where baseball card copies will be placed.

6 Place card copy on decoupaged part of box. Using your fingers, smooth into place. Paint another layer of decoupage glue over card.

7 Repeat Steps 5–6 for all cards. *Glue several card copies over box opening. Let dry. Slice through them with a craft knife, so that the box opens.* Paint layer of decoupage glue over the whole surface of box.

Step 7

8 Paint decoupage glue over baseballs. Let dry for 30 minutes.

9 Apply small amount of wood glue to flat bottom of four baseballs. Place onto bottom of box. *You've just created feet for your box.*

10 Apply small amount of wood glue to remaining baseball. Place onto center of lid. *You've just created a handle.*

11 Using old toothbrush, **Spatter** box with black acrylic paint.

Spatter

1. Using old toothbrush, dip bristles into paint that has been slightly thinned with water.

2. Hold toothbrush about 6"–8" away from box with bristles pointed towards box. Draw your finger or thumb toward you across bristles, causing paint to spatter onto box.

Step 11

Labels & Tags

Personalize your projects by creating labels and tags for them. Let the labels and tags reflect your personality. They can include your name, the date, or a special message. Place the label on the back of your projects so that the person you gave the project to will always remember that it came from you. If the project is for you, use a label with a date so that you will remember when it was created.

Labels and tags can be made from adhesive-backed paper, card stock, or decorative paper. You can decorate them with stickers, glitter, or stamped images.

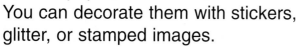

Metric Conversion Chart

mm-millimetres cm-centimetres
inches to millimetres and centimetres

inches	mm	cm	inches	cm	inches	cm
⅛	3	0.3	9	22.9	30	76.2
¼	6	0.6	10	25.4	31	78.7
⅜	10	1.0	11	27.9	32	81.3
½	13	1.3	12	30.5	33	83.8
⅝	16	1.6	13	33.0	34	86.4
¾	19	1.9	14	35.6	35	88.9
⅞	22	2.2	15	38.1	36	91.4
1	25	2.5	16	40.6	37	94.0
1¼	32	3.2	17	43.2	38	96.5
1½	38	3.8	18	45.7	39	99.1
1¾	44	4.4	19	48.3	40	101.6
2	51	5.1	20	50.8	41	104.1
2½	64	6.4	21	53.3	42	106.7
3	76	7.6	22	55.9	43	109.2
3½	89	8.9	23	58.4	44	111.8
4	102	10.2	24	61.0	45	114.3
4½	114	11.4	25	63.5	46	116.8
5	127	12.7	26	66.0	47	119.4
6	152	15.2	27	68.6	48	121.9
7	178	17.8	28	71.1	49	124.5
8	203	20.3	29	73.7	50	127.0

yards to metres

yards	metres	yards	metres	yards	metres	yards	metres	yards	metres
⅛	0.11	2⅛	1.94	4⅛	3.77	6⅛	5.60	8⅛	7.43
¼	0.23	2¼	2.06	4¼	3.89	6¼	5.72	8¼	7.54
⅜	0.34	2⅜	2.17	4⅜	4.00	6⅜	5.83	8⅜	7.66
½	0.46	2½	2.29	4½	4.11	6½	5.94	8½	7.77
⅝	0.57	2⅝	2.40	4⅝	4.23	6⅝	6.06	8⅝	7.89
¾	0.69	2¾	2.51	4¾	4.34	6¾	6.17	8¾	8.00
⅞	0.80	2⅞	2.63	4⅞	4.46	6⅞	6.29	8⅞	8.12
1	0.91	3	2.74	5	4.57	7	6.40	9	8.23
1⅛	1.03	3⅛	2.86	5⅛	4.69	7⅛	6.52	9⅛	8.34
1¼	1.14	3¼	2.97	5¼	4.80	7¼	6.63	9¼	8.46
1⅜	1.26	3⅜	3.09	5⅜	4.91	7⅜	6.74	9⅜	8.57
1½	1.37	3½	3.20	5½	5.03	7½	6.86	9½	8.69
1⅝	1.49	3⅝	3.31	5⅝	5.14	7⅝	6.97	9⅝	8.80
1¾	1.60	3¾	3.43	5¾	5.26	7¾	7.09	9¾	8.92
1⅞	1.71	3⅞	3.54	5⅞	5.37	7⅞	7.20	9⅞	9.03
2	1.83	4	3.66	6	5.49	8	7.32	10	9.14

Where to Look